CELEBRATING THE NAME WILLIAM

Celebrating the Name William

Walter the Educator

Silent King Books a WhichHead Imprint

Copyright © 2024 by Walter the Educator

All rights reserved. No part of this book may be reproduced in any manner whatsoever without written permission except in the case of brief quotations embodied in critical articles and reviews.

First Printing, 2024

Disclaimer
This book is a literary work; poems are not about specific persons, locations, situations, and/or circumstances unless mentioned in a historical context. This book is for entertainment and informational purposes only. The author and publisher offer this information without warranties expressed or implied. No matter the grounds, neither the author nor the publisher will be accountable for any losses, injuries, or other damages caused by the reader's use of this book. The use of this book acknowledges an understanding and acceptance of this disclaimer.

dedicated to everyone with the first name of William

CONTENTS

Dedication v

One - Name So Strong 1

Two - Mighty Roar 3

Three - Name Of Gold 5

Four - Dear William 7

Five - Name Of Courage 9

Six - Celebrate The Name William 11

Seven - Testament To Will 13

Eight - Touches The Sky 15

Nine - Every Allure 17

Ten - Regal And Grand 19

Eleven - History And Legacy 21

Twelve - Reign Supreme 23

Thirteen - Defines The Best 25

Fourteen - Strong And Strong	. . . . . .	27
Fifteen - From William	. . . . . .	29
Sixteen - Ancient Lore	. . . . .	31
Seventeen - Raise A Cheer	. . . . .	33
Eighteen - Name Of Power	. . . .	35
Nineteen - Hail To Thee	. . . . .	37
Twenty - Takes The Lead	. . . . .	39
Twenty-One - Noble Deeds	. . . . .	41
Twenty-Two - Depths Of The Heart	. . . . .	43
Twenty-Three - Soul Of The Land	. . . . .	45
Twenty-Four - Strength Divine	. . . . .	47
Twenty-Five - Resolute And Still	. . . . .	49
Twenty-Six - Symphony Of Syllables	. . . .	51
Twenty-Seven - Source Of Inspiration	. . . .	53
Twenty-Eight - Radiant Star	. . . . .	55
Twenty-Nine - Priceless Worth	. . . . .	57
Thirty - Winds Of Destiny	. . . .	59
Thirty-One - I Trust In You	. . . .	61
Thirty-Two - Harmony	. . . .	63
Thirty-Three - Name So Rare	. . . . . .	65

Thirty-Four - Again And Again 67

Thirty-Five - William Sparkles 69

About The Creator 71

ONE

NAME SO STRONG

Oh, William, with a name so strong,
In your honor, we sing this song.
A name of old, with a timeless grace,
In every heart, you find your place.

In fields of green and skies so wide,
Your name echoes, a joyful stride.
With every breath, a tale you tell,
Of ancient lore, where legends dwell.

William, a name that stands so tall,
In history's pages, you never fall.
A beacon bright, in the darkest night,
Guiding souls with pure delight.

From hills to valleys, your name resounds,
In whispered winds and joyful sounds.
A name of honor, a name of might,
In every heart, you shine so bright.

So let us raise our voices high,
And praise the name that fills the sky.
For William, oh, so grand and true,
This ode to you, we gladly brew.

In every land, in every tongue,
Your name is spoken, forever young.
Oh, William, with a name so fine,
In every verse, you brightly shine.

TWO

MIGHTY ROAR

William, a name that echoes through the ages,
In history's tapestry, it's been penned for ages.
A moniker of strength and noble might,
In every heart, it shines so bright.

With syllables that dance upon the lips,
In every story, your name equips.
A legacy of honor, a legacy of grace,
In every corner, your presence we trace.

From ancient castles to modern streets,
In every heartbeat, your rhythm beats.
A name that carries tales untold,
In whispers of the young and the old.

In fields of valor and battles of yore,
Your name resounds with a mighty roar.
A symbol of courage, a symbol of will,
In every dream, you linger still.

William, a name that stands the test of time,
In every era, it's at its prime.
So let us raise our voices high,
And praise this name that fills the sky.

For in this world, and the next one too,
William, we celebrate the essence of you.
A name that holds a universe of might,
In every soul, you take flight.

THREE

NAME OF GOLD

In the land of rolling hills and golden fields,
There lived a man named William, strong and true.
With eyes like sapphires and a heart that yields,
He walked with purpose, in all that he'd pursue.

William, oh William, a name so grand,
It echoes through the ages, a timeless sound.
In every corner of this wondrous land,
It's a name that's cherished, for it knows no bound.

From the bustling cities to the quiet glades,
William's name resounds in every place.
It weaves through stories and ancient ballads,
A name of honor, dignity, and grace.

As the stars twinkle in the midnight sky,
So does the name of William, shining bright.
A beacon of hope, soaring ever high,
Guiding lost souls through the darkest night.

So let us raise our voices, let us proclaim,
The name of William, let it be known.
For in its essence, it holds eternal flame,
A name that's cherished, proudly shown.

Oh William, dear William, your name we sing,
In melodies sweet and tales of old.
For in your name, a legacy takes wing,
A name of valor, a name of gold.

FOUR

DEAR WILLIAM

In the realm of dreams and whispered lore,
Dwells a soul named William, forevermore.
With a gaze that kindles fires, a spirit pure,
He treads the earth, his presence sure.

William, oh William, a symphony in sound,
A name that echoes through history's ground.
From ancient castles to modern streets,
It weaves through time, in endless beats.

In the heart of nature, where rivers flow,
And mountains stand tall, covered in snow,
William's name dances on the breeze,
A tribute to strength, and boundless ease.

In the depths of silence, where secrets lie,
And stars paint the canvas of the sky,
William's name glimmers with timeless grace,
A legacy woven in time and space.

So let us raise our voices, let us extol,
The name of William, a legend to enroll.
For in its essence, it holds a mystic charm,
A name that shields from all harm.

Oh William, dear William, your name we hail,
In verses of old and tales that prevail.
For in your name, a legacy takes flight,
A name of honor, a name of might.

FIVE

NAME OF COURAGE

In the whispers of the wind and the rustling trees,
Resides a figure named William, with a heart at ease.
With eyes that sparkle like the morning dew,
He walks the earth, steadfast and true.

William, oh William, a symphony of strength,
A name that resonates, no matter the length.
From ancient legends to modern days,
It echoes through time in endless ways.

In the embrace of the ocean's mighty roar,
And the gentle lull of the shore,
William's name carries a timeless embrace,
A symbol of resilience, boundless grace.

In the heart of adventure, where dreams take flight,
And the stars guide the wanderer through the night,
William's name shines with unwavering light,
A beacon of hope, burning ever bright.

So let us raise our voices, let us celebrate,
The name of William, noble and great.
For in its essence, it holds a sacred power,
A name that weaves through every hour.
Oh William, dear William, your name we adore,
In melodies sweet and epics of yore.
For in your name, a legacy unfurls,
A name of courage, a name that whirls.

SIX

CELEBRATE THE NAME WILLIAM

In the heart of the forest, where the ancient trees stand tall,
There lies a whispering breeze, calling out the name William.
A name as mighty as the oak, enduring through the ages,
A name that echoes through the canyons, strong and courageous.

William, like the river flowing with wisdom and grace,
Carving through the earth, leaving a lasting trace.
As resilient as the mountains, steadfast and true,
A name that blooms like wildflowers, in every shade and hue.

In the fields of gold, where the sun kisses the earth,

The name William shines bright, a beacon of infinite worth.
Like the stars that adorn the midnight sky, a constellation of hope,
Guiding wayfarers through the darkness, helping them to cope.

William, a melody that resonates through the meadows and hills,
A name that dances with the wind, bringing joy and thrills.
As vibrant as the rainbow after a gentle rain,
A name that weaves through nature's tapestry, never in vain.

So let us raise our voices, like the birds in the sky,
And celebrate the name William, soaring high and nigh.
For in this world of wonders, where nature's beauty thrills,
The name William stands out, like a mountain among the hills.

SEVEN

TESTAMENT TO WILL

In the realm of dreams, where fantasies take flight,
Resides a name so grand, William, a beacon of might.
Like the phoenix rising from ashes, with fiery allure,
William ignites the soul, a name so pure.

In the garden of life, where diversity blooms,
William blossoms as a rare and precious heirloom.
A name that sparkles like dew on a petal at dawn,
Enchanting all with its grace, from dusk until dawn.

William, a symphony of notes that linger in the air,
A name that whispers secrets, with an enigmatic flair.
Like the moon casting its glow upon the tranquil sea,
William reflects serenity, in its essence so free.

In the tapestry of time, where destinies entwine,
William stands as a legend, a name so divine.
As enduring as the oak, with roots deep and strong,
William weathers every storm, where it truly belongs.

So let us raise a toast, to this name so bold and true,
William, a masterpiece in a world so new.
For in the kaleidoscope of existence, where colors blend and spill,
The name William shines bright, a testament to will.

EIGHT

TOUCHES THE SKY

Oh, William, a moniker so grand,
In its sound, a melody that does expand,
Like a river flowing with grace,
Emanating strength and poise in its embrace.

From ancient times to modern days,
The name William always holds its praise,
A beacon of honor and noble might,
Guiding souls through the darkest night.

In letters formed, a symphony of art,
Each curve and line, a work of heart,
A name that echoes through the ages,
In history's boundless, eternal pages.

William, a name of regal air,
A legacy that's beyond compare,
In every syllable, a tale untold,
Of bravery, wisdom, and stories bold.

So let us raise our voices high,
And sing the name that touches the sky,
For in the realm of names so true,
William, we celebrate the beauty of you.

NINE

EVERY ALLURE

William, a name that echoes through time,
In its essence, a rhythm so sublime,
Like the dance of autumn leaves in the breeze,
Or the whisper of waves on tranquil seas.

A symphony of syllables, a cadence rare,
In each letter, a legacy to declare,
Of kings and knights, of valor and might,
A name that shines in the darkest night.

In the tapestry of history, it weaves,
A name that perseveres and achieves,
From Shakespeare's quill to modern days,
William, a name that forever stays.

In the gardens of language, it blooms,
A name that resonates, never consumes,
The echoes of courage and wisdom untold,
In the name William, a story unfolds.

So let's raise our voices and sing,
Of the name that carries a majestic ring,
For in every William, a tale resides,
Of strength, of honor, where love abides.
   In the realm of names, it stands tall,
A beacon of hope, a clarion call,
William, a name that will endure,
In every heartbeat, in every allure.

TEN

REGAL AND GRAND

William, a name so regal and grand,
In history and lore, it takes a stand.
From William the Conqueror to Shakespeare's quill,
This name exudes strength and an iron will.

In fields of battle, a William's might,
Leading armies to victory, shining bright.
With courage and honor, they stand tall,
Their name echoing through the ages, never to fall.

William, a name of wisdom and grace,
In every challenge, they find their place.
From the depths of despair to the heights of success,
They navigate life's journey with finesse.

In the world of art, a William's touch,
Creates masterpieces that impress so much.
Their creativity knows no bounds,
Innovating and inspiring, their art astounds.

William, a name that stands the test of time,
A beacon of hope in every clime.
So here's to the William, strong and true,
This poem celebrates the greatness of you.

ELEVEN

HISTORY AND LEGACY

In the vast expanse of time, a name was forged
A name that echoes through the ages, William
It carries the weight of history and legacy
A name that stands tall, unwavering and strong
William, a name like a mighty oak tree
Rooted in tradition, yet reaching for the sky
It sings of courage, honor, and valor
A name that commands respect and admiration
In the tapestry of life, William is a thread
Weaving through the fabric of humanity
A name that resonates with power and grace
Eternal and timeless, like the stars above
William, a name that dances on the wind
Whispered in the rustling leaves of ancient forests
It holds the secrets of generations past
A name that speaks of wisdom and knowledge

    When spoken, William ignites a flame
A flame that illuminates the darkest night
It ignites passion, ambition, and determination
A name that fuels the fires of greatness
    So let us raise our voices and celebrate
The name of William, a symphony of strength
A name that will endure for all eternity
A name that will never fade, but only grow brighter

TWELVE

REIGN SUPREME

In the realm of names, a gem shines bright
William, a beacon of splendor and might
It conjures images of chivalry and grace
A name that stands tall in history's embrace
William, like a river flowing free
Carving its path through the landscape of time
It whispers tales of valor and might
A name that echoes with an ancient rhyme
In the garden of names, William blooms
A rare and precious flower, rich in hues
It paints a picture of strength and resilience
A name that weaves a tapestry of brilliance
William, like a symphony in the air
Melodic and grand, a timeless affair
It sings of courage and noble deeds
A name that plants the boldest of seeds

    When William is spoken, the earth stands still
A name that carries the weight of a quill
Inscribe in history, in letters bold and grand
A name that will forever proudly stand
    So let us raise our voices high and true
In honor of William, noble and true
A name that will forever reign supreme
A name that will forever gleam

THIRTEEN

DEFINES THE BEST

In the tapestry of names, William shines
A beacon of strength, woven in timeless lines
It resonates with echoes of ancient lore
A name that stands firm, forevermore
  William, like a mountain standing tall
Majestic and resolute, it heeds the call
It echoes tales of valor and might
A name that ignites the spirit's light
  In the symphony of words, William sings
A melody of honor, like golden wings
It soars through the annals of history
A name that embodies boundless mystery
  William, like a phoenix rising high
From the ashes of time, it takes to the sky
It symbolizes resilience and grace
A name that leaves an indelible trace

When William is uttered, the world takes heed
A name that plants the courage seed
It speaks of legacy, noble and true
A name that echoes through the ages, anew
So let us raise our voices in jubilation
For the name of William, a timeless sensation
A name that will forever stand the test
A name that eternally defines the best

FOURTEEN

STRONG AND STRONG

William, a name of strength and might
A moniker that shines so bright
It carries with it history and grace
A name that time cannot erase
    In ancient times, it stood the test
A name that's truly been the best
From battles fought to kingdoms won
William's legacy is never done
    With syllables that roll like thunder
In every land, it's a name to wonder
From William the Conqueror to the Bard
This name has traveled near and far
    In gardens, courts, and halls of fame
William's presence is never tame
It echoes through the halls of time
A name that's truly so sublime

So here's to William, bold and true
A name that's old yet ever new
In every heart, it leaves its mark
A name that shines through light and dark
So raise a glass, let's all cheer
For William, a name so dear
Let it ring through the ages long
A name that's forever strong and strong

FIFTEEN

FROM WILLIAM

Oh, William, a name that's grand and true
With letters that dance in the morning dew
It carries a melody that sings so clear
A name that banishes all fear
From William the wise to the daring knight
This name shines in the brightest light
It echoes through the hills and vales
Leaving behind its glorious trails
In every land, it stands so tall
A name that's cherished by one and all
With each syllable, a tale untold
Of bravery and stories yet to unfold
From William the thinker to the gallant heart
This name has played its noble part
In every epic, it finds its place
A name that time cannot erase

 So here's to William, so full of might
A name that conquers the darkest night
It weaves through history's sacred loom
A name that banishes all gloom
 So let's raise our voices high
For William, a name that touches the sky
Let it soar through the endless blue
A name that's forever bold and true

SIXTEEN

ANCIENT LORE

    William, a name of ancient lore
Resonating through time and more
A symphony in syllables, so grand
Echoing across the timeless land
    From William the conqueror to the poet's quill
This name holds stories that give us chills
A name that speaks of bravery and might
Guiding us through the darkest night
    In every battle, it stands so tall
A name that heeds the warrior's call
With each letter, a legacy unfolds
Of honor and tales yet to be told
    From William the leader to the noble soul
This name has left its immortal scroll
In every epic, it finds its place
A name that time cannot erase

    So here's to William, bold and free
A name that echoes through history
Let it ring through the ages long
A name that's forever brave and strong
    So raise a cheer, let it resound
For William, a name so profound
Let it soar through the boundless sky
A name that will never die

SEVENTEEN

RAISE A CHEER

William, a name that echoes through the ages
In history's boundless pages
A symphony of syllables, so grand
Guiding us through the timeless land
From William the wise to the gallant knight
This name shines with a radiant light
It weaves through tales of honor and might
A name that banishes the darkest night
In every kingdom, it stands so tall
A name that answers the noble call
With each letter, a legend untold
Of bravery and stories yet to unfold
From William the conqueror to the poet's verse
This name holds tales that never disperse
In every epic, it finds its place
A name that time cannot erase

So here's to William, so full of grace
A name that time cannot efface
Let it ring through the ages long
A name that's forever bold and strong
So raise a cheer, let it resound
For William, a name so renowned
Let it soar through the endless sky
A name that will never say goodbye

EIGHTEEN

NAME OF POWER

Oh William, a name so bold and strong,
In history, it's been cherished long.
From William the Conqueror to Shakespeare's quill,
This name has always held great skill.

In battlefields and on the stage,
The name William has adorned many a page.
With wisdom and courage, it stands tall,
A name that echoes through the hall.

William, a name of noble grace,
In every challenge, it finds its place.
With each syllable, a story untold,
A tale of bravery, so bold and old.

From William Wallace to William Tell,
The name has stories to retell.
In every corner of the earth,
The name William carries great worth.

So raise a glass to William's name,
In every triumph and every claim.
For in this name, there lies a tale,
Of strength and honor that will never pale.
　　Oh William, a name that never fades,
In every forest and in every glade.
A name of power, a name of might,
In the realm of names, it shines so bright.

NINETEEN

HAIL TO THEE

Hail to thee, William, a name so grand,
In every land, across the sand.
From ancient times to modern days,
Your resonance echoes in endless ways.

William, a moniker of regal acclaim,
In every era, it builds its frame.
From royal courts to common folk,
It's a name that no chains can yoke.

In letters and verses, it finds its home,
In every verse, it loves to roam.
With syllables that dance and entwine,
In the world of names, it's a precious shrine.

From William the Silent to William the Wise,
The name holds tales that mesmerize.
In every heart, it plants a seed,
A legacy that no one can impede.

Oh, William, a beacon of strength and might,
In every battle, it shines so bright.
With honor and courage, it leads the way,
A name that never goes astray.

So here's to William, so bold and true,
In every sky, in every hue.
A name that weaves a timeless song,
In the tapestry of words, it belongs.

TWENTY

TAKES THE LEAD

Hail, oh William, a name so dear,
In every whisper, in every cheer.
From ancient times to the present day,
Your presence glows in a timeless way.

William, a name of valor and might,
In every realm, it shines so bright.
From tales of old to legends anew,
It holds a power that continues to imbue.

In history's tapestry, it weaves its thread,
A name that never bows its head.
From William the Bold to William the Free,
It echoes through time, for all to see.

Oh, William, a symphony of strength and grace,
In every challenge, it finds its place.
With honor and wisdom, it leads the throng,
A name that resonates, bold and strong.

From William the Conqueror to William the True,
The name holds stories, both old and new.
In every heart, it plants its seed,
A legacy that forever takes the lead.

So here's to William, a name of renown,
In every smile, in every frown.
A name that paints a vivid scene,
In the gallery of names, it reigns supreme.

TWENTY-ONE

NOBLE DEEDS

Oh, William, your name rings with regal grace,
A moniker of strength and timeless embrace.
In ancient lore and modern tale,
Your name stands tall, it will never fail.

From William the Conqueror to the bard of Stratford town,
Your name echoes through history, wearing a golden crown.
In fields of battle and halls of art,
William, your name plays a leading part.

With syllables that dance and letters that sing,
William, your name is a powerful thing.
It carries the weight of noble deeds,
And fills the heart with gallant needs.

Oh, William, in every letter and every sound,
Your name holds a promise, solid and profound.

In every sunrise and every night,
William, your name shines with a radiant light.
    So, let us raise our voices high,
And honor William, the name that will never die.
In poetry, in song, in tales that we tell,
William, your name weaves a magical spell.

TWENTY-TWO

DEPTHS OF THE HEART

Oh, William, your name is a symphony of syllables,
A tapestry of letters woven into noble quills.
In the garden of names, yours blooms like a grand rose,
With petals of history and thorns of prose.

From William the wordsmith to the warrior of old,
Your name carries tales that will never grow cold.
In the chronicles of time and the whispers of fate,
William, your name stands strong and great.

With each letter, a melody, with each sound, a story,
William, your name paints a portrait of glory.
In the dance of language and the song of the soul,
Your name resonates like a timeless toll.

Oh, William, in every echo and every verse,
Your name holds a legacy, a blessing, a curse.

In the annals of honor and the depths of the heart,
William, your name is a work of art.
    So, let us raise our voices and lift our pens,
And celebrate William, among noble women and men.
In the ballads we sing and the legends we weave,
William, your name reigns, and it will never leave.

TWENTY-THREE

SOUL OF THE LAND

William, oh William, a name of ancient might,
A symphony of syllables, a beacon in the night.
In the tapestry of time, your name stands tall,
A fortress of honor, never to fall.

From William the wise to the wanderer of old,
Your name tells stories, timeless and bold.
In the ballads of bravery and the whispers of lore,
William, your name shines forevermore.

With each letter, a brushstroke, with each sound, a song,
William, your name dances, elegant and strong.
In the melody of existence and the rhythm of fate,
Your name echoes like a celestial gate.

Oh, William, in every verse and every rhyme,
Your name holds a power, ancient and prime.

In the heart of legends and the soul of the land,
William, your name is an enduring strand.
 So, let us raise our voices and honor your name,
In the chronicles of courage and the halls of fame.
In the verses we write and the dreams we fulfill,
William, your name lingers, steadfast and still.

TWENTY-FOUR

STRENGTH DIVINE

William, oh William, a name that echoes through time,
A symphony of syllables, a mountain to climb.
In the tapestry of tales, your name takes flight,
A legacy of valor, shining bright.

From William the warrior to the weaver of dreams,
Your name holds the power of celestial streams.
In the whispers of history and the songs of yore,
William, your name opens every door.

With each letter, a melody, with each sound, a story,
William, your name paints a picture of glory.
In the dance of destiny and the embrace of the soul,
Your name resonates like a timeless scroll.

Oh, William, in every verse and every line,
Your name holds the essence of strength divine.

In the heart of legends and the spirit of lore,
William, your name is an eternal core.
So, let us raise our voices and sing your praise,
In the ballads of honor and the sun's gentle rays.
In the verses we craft and the tales we unfurl,
William, your name remains a timeless pearl.

TWENTY-FIVE

RESOLUTE AND STILL

William, oh William, a name of ancient lore,
A tapestry of syllables, a legend to explore.
In the chronicles of time, your name stands tall,
A fortress of bravery, never to fall.

From William the wise to the wanderer of old,
Your name weaves tales, timeless and bold.
In the ballads of courage and the whispers of the wind,
William, your name echoes, a legacy enshrined.

With each letter, a brushstroke, with each sound, a tale,
William, your name dances, beyond the earthly veil.
In the melody of existence and the rhythm of the heart,
Your name resonates like a timeless work of art.

Oh, William, in every verse and every rhyme,

Your name holds a power, enduring and prime.
In the heart of legends and the spirit of the land,
William, your name stands, a monument grand.

So, let us raise our voices and honor your name,
In the chronicles of history and the halls of fame.
In the verses we write and the dreams we fulfill,
William, your name lingers, resolute and still.

TWENTY-SIX

SYMPHONY OF SYLLABLES

William, a name like a sturdy oak,
Rooted in history, its branches evoke
Strength and resilience, standing tall and true,
Weathering storms, a symbol of virtue.

Like a compass guiding ships at sea,
William's name steers through uncertainty,
A beacon of wisdom, a steady hand,
Navigating life's intricate strand.

In the tapestry of time, William's name
Is a golden thread, woven without shame,
Binding stories of valor and might,
A legacy glowing in the darkest night.

As a phoenix rising from ash and flame,
William's name ignites an eternal flame,

Burning with passion, never to tire,
A symbol of hope, a relentless fire.
    Oh, William, your name is an endless song,
A melody that lingers, powerful and strong,
A symphony of syllables, a timeless art,
Engraved in the depths of every heart.

TWENTY-SEVEN

SOURCE OF INSPIRATION

William, like a majestic eagle in flight,
Soaring through the skies with grace and might,
Your name embodies freedom's endless call,
A symbol of courage, standing proud and tall.

As steady as a lighthouse on the shore,
Guiding ships through tempests and more,
William's name shines with unwavering light,
A beacon of hope, through the darkest night.

Like a river flowing with wisdom's embrace,
William's name navigates time and space,
Carving paths of knowledge, deep and wide,
A source of inspiration, a boundless guide.

As resilient as an ancient oak tree,
William's name stands strong, noble and free,

Rooted in history, yet reaching for the sky,
A testament to honor that will never die.
    Oh, William, your name is a symphony of grace,
A tapestry of tales from every time and place,
A legacy that flourishes, steadfast and pure,
An emblem of strength that will endure.

TWENTY-EIGHT

RADIANT STAR

William, like a radiant star in the night sky,
Your name shines with brilliance, soaring high,
A celestial body of timeless allure,
Guiding souls with a steadfast, radiant pure.

As bold as a lion ruling the plains,
William's name echoes with majestic refrains,
A regal presence, commanding and strong,
In the realm of names, it eternally belongs.

Like a grand oak, weathered by centuries past,
William's name stands unwavering, steadfast,
Roots delving deep into history's embrace,
A symbol of endurance, an everlasting grace.

As resilient as the mountains, ancient and wise,
William's name reaches for the boundless skies,
A symbol of strength, unyielding and grand,
In the symphony of names, a timeless band.

William's impact on the world is profound,
A legacy of honor, forever renowned,
A name that resonates through history's halls,
Inspiring greatness, as the world recalls.

Oh, William, your name is a symphony of grace,
A tapestry of tales from every time and place,
A legacy that flourishes, steadfast and pure,
An emblem of strength that will endure.

TWENTY-NINE

PRICELESS WORTH

Oh, William, thy name doth carry grace,
A moniker of strength and noble trace.
In fields of green and skies of blue,
Thy name doth echo, pure and true.

With every syllable, a tale untold,
Of bravery and wisdom, a spirit bold.
In the whispers of the wind, it's heard,
A name that's cherished, like a precious bird.

William, a name that stands the test,
Of time and trials, it's truly blessed.
In every letter, a story unfolds,
Of victories won and tales untold.

From mountains high to valleys low,
Thy name resounds, a radiant glow.
In every corner of the earth,
Thy name brings joy and priceless worth.

Oh, William, in every language spoken,
Thy name remains unbroken, unshaken.
A symphony of sounds, a melody divine,
In every heart, thy name will shine.
   So here's to William, a name so grand,
A beacon of hope in every land.
May it echo through eternity,
A name of beauty and serenity.

THIRTY

WINDS OF DESTINY

Hail, William, a name of regal charm,
A symphony of letters, a soothing balm.
In the tapestry of time, it gleams,
A name that inspires, a name that dreams.

With each consonant and vowel in place,
William, a name of elegance and grace.
In the dance of words, it takes its flight,
A name that shines in the darkest night.

From ancient castles to modern streets,
William's name, a melody that beats.
In every heartbeat, a rhythm so true,
A name that whispers, "I believe in you."

Oh, William, in every corner of the earth,
A name of valor, of immeasurable worth.
In the echoes of history, it stands tall,
A name that weaves a timeless thrall.

Through trials and triumphs, it stands strong,
William, a name like a comforting song.
In the gardens of language, it blooms,
A name that dispels all worldly glooms.

So here's to William, a name so rare,
A name that carries a dignified air.
May it soar through the winds of destiny,
A name of hope, of boundless harmony.

THIRTY-ONE

I TRUST IN YOU

    Hail, William, a name that sparkles bright,
A beacon of hope, a guiding light.
In the tapestry of life, it weaves,
A name that inspires, a name that achieves.
    With every syllable, a tale unfolds,
Of courage and kindness, it beholds.
In the whispers of the breeze, it sings,
A name that uplifts, a name that brings.
    William, a name that stands so bold,
In history's pages, it's firmly strolled.
In every letter, a story is told,
Of bravery and honor, a spirit so bold.
    From ancient lands to modern scenes,
William's name, a vision so serene.
In every heart, a melody rings true,
A name that echoes, "I trust in you."

Oh, William, in every language spoken,
A name that won't ever be broken.
A symphony of sounds, a harmony divine,
In every soul, thy name will shine.

So here's to William, a name so grand,
A name that echoes across the land.
May it rise in the tides of eternity,
A name of beauty and endless serenity.

THIRTY-TWO

HARMONY

Hail, William, a name of ancient lore,
A symphony of letters, a name to adore.
In the tapestry of time, it gleams,
A name that inspires, a name that dreams.

With every consonant and vowel in place,
William, a name of elegance and grace.
In the dance of words, it takes its flight,
A name that shines in the darkest night.

From towering peaks to tranquil streams,
William's name, a melody that gleams.
In every heartbeat, a rhythm so true,
A name that whispers, "I believe in you."

Oh, William, in every corner of the earth,
A name of valor, of immeasurable worth.
In the echoes of history, it stands tall,
A name that weaves a timeless thrall.

Through trials and triumphs, it stands strong,
William, a name like a comforting song.
In the gardens of language, it blooms,
A name that dispels all worldly glooms.

So here's to William, a name so rare,
A name that carries a dignified air.
May it soar through the winds of destiny,
A name of hope, of boundless harmony.

THIRTY-THREE

NAME SO RARE

Hail, William, a name of ancient lore,
A symphony of letters, a name to adore.
In the tapestry of time, it gleams,
A name that inspires, a name that dreams.
From the days of knights and medieval lore,
To the Renaissance's cultural uproar,
William's name, a melody that's been,
Through the ages, a timeless sheen.
From the reign of Charlemagne to the Magna Carta's scene,
William's name, a melody that's been.
In every heartbeat, a rhythm so true,
A name that whispers, "I believe in you."
Oh, William, in every corner of the earth,
A name of valor, of immeasurable worth.

In the echoes of history, it stands tall,
A name that weaves a timeless thrall.
   Through the Crusades and the Age of Enlightenment's bloom,
William, a name like a comforting tune.
In the gardens of language, it blooms,
A name that dispels all worldly glooms.
   So here's to William, a name so rare,
A name that carries a dignified air.
May it soar through the winds of destiny,
A name of hope, of boundless harmony.

THIRTY-FOUR

AGAIN AND AGAIN

In the realm of nomenclature, William stands tall,
A moniker revered, echoing in every hall.
A name, resplendent in its syllabic grace,
In life's grand tapestry, it finds its place.

William, a symphony of letters, a linguistic dance,
In the lexicon of existence, a name of chance.
Whispers of the willow, rustling leaves spell the tale,
A name that weaves through history's gale.

In the celestial dance, a star named William gleams,
Illuminating the night with its celestial beams.
A cognomen like no other, a beacon in the dark,
In the symposium of names, it leaves its mark.

Through epochs and eras, a timeless echo,
A moniker of strength, where virtues grow.
In the garden of language, William blossoms fair,
A perennial word, beyond compare.

Oh, William, a sonnet in every sound,
In the vast lexicon, your echoes abound.
A name that dances on the poet's pen,
In the anthology of life, again and again.

THIRTY-FIVE

WILLIAM SPARKLES

In the cosmic ballet of appellations, William takes its stand,
A resplendent gem in the lexicon, a symphony grand.
With syllables that waltz, a linguistic ballet,
In the tapestry of language, it paints its display.

William, a majestic river flowing through time,
A melodic sonnet, an eloquent rhyme.
In the mosaic of letters, it gleams like a star,
A name whispered by zephyrs from lands afar.

Through the corridors of history, William strides,
A moniker with depth, where courage abides.
Echoes of valor in each uttered syllable,
A name that resonates, unyielding and stable.

In the celestial dance, a comet's bright trail,
William sparkles, leaving an indelible tale.

A cosmic lyric in the vast verse of life,
A name with cadence, amid joy and strife.
   Oh, William, a phoenix in the linguistic fire,
In the lexicon's symposium, you inspire.
A harmonious echo in the poet's quill,
In the anthology of words, you linger still.

ABOUT THE CREATOR

Walter the Educator is one of the pseudonyms for Walter Anderson. Formally educated in Chemistry, Business, and Education, he is an educator, an author, a diverse entrepreneur, and he is the son of a disabled war veteran. "Walter the Educator" shares his time between educating and creating. He holds interests and owns several creative projects that entertain, enlighten, enhance, and educate, hoping to inspire and motivate you.

Follow, find new works, and stay up to date
with Walter the Educator™
at WaltertheEducator.com

www.ingramcontent.com/pod-product-compliance
Lightning Source LLC
LaVergne TN
LVHW052000060526
838201LV00059B/3759